THE HOUSE & GARDEN BOOK OF
Classic Rooms

ROBERT HARLING·LEONIE HIGHTON·JOHN BRIDGES

THE HOUSE & GARDEN BOOK OF
Classic Rooms

ROBERT HARLING · LEONIE HIGHTON · JOHN BRIDGES

The Vendome Press
NEW YORK

Acknowledgements

Many of the rooms illustrated in this book were researched by Lavinia Bolton and Sally Griffiths.

Photographs: Simon Brown 6 (top), 10–11, 14–15, 28–29, 44–45, 52–53, 70–71, 78–79, 84–85, 148–151, 154–155, 180–181, 190–191, 194–195, 204–205, 212–213, 220–221; Jacques Dirand 218–219; Michael Dunne 208–209; Andreas von Einsiedel 82–83, 146–147, 164–165, 192–193, 196–197; David Massey 7 (top), 8 (bottom), 34–35, 42–43, 46–47, 60–61, 64–65, 72–73, 76–77, 92–95, 152–153, 160–161, 182–183; James Mortimer 132–133; Ianthe Ruthven 7 (bottom), 100–101; Fritz von der Schulenburg 2–3, 6 (bottom), 7 (middle), 8 (top and middle), 9 (top and bottom), 12–13, 16–17, 30–33, 36–41, 48–51, 54–59, 62–63, 66–69, 74–75, 80–81, 86–91, 96–99, 102–131, 134–145, 156–159, 162–163, 166–179, 184–189, 198–203, 206–207, 210–211, 214–217, 222–223, 224.

Published in the United States and Canada
by The Vendome Press
515 Madison Avenue
New York City
10022

Distributed in the USA and Canada by
Rizzoli International Publications
through St. Martin's Press
175 Fifth Avenue
New York, NY 10010

First Published in 1989 by
Chatto & Windus Ltd
London

Library of Congress Cataloging-in-Publication Data

Harling, Robert,
The House & Garden book of classic rooms/by Robert
Harling, Leonie Highton, John Bridges.
p.   cm.
ISBN 0–86565–118–3
1. Interior decoration.   I. Highton, Leonie.   II. Bridges, John.
III. Title.   IV. Title: House and garden book of classic rooms.
NK2175.H37   1990
747—dc20   89–38743
                                                              CIP

Printed and bound in Singapore

Contents

Introduction   6

Arcadian retreats   10

Gorgeous colour   40

Glamorous reflections   60

Panelled patinas   74

Print-rooms revived   100

Eccentric spaces   114

Grander windows   138

En-suite   160

Flexible stripes   178

Dining with panache   200

That word 'classic'

Arcadian retreats: *the English country-house look at Sudeley Castle (page 10).*

Gorgeous colour: *vivid coral-red walls as a background for entertaining (page 40).*

'Classic' is one of the most obliging, flexible and misunderstood words in the English language, frequently used to approve a building, a musical performance, physical beauty or even, at a pinch, an agreeable wine.

Yet, thanks to our deference to academics, we are apt to think of 'classic' as relating particularly to the literature, drama, history, mythology and architecture of the ancient Greeks and Romans. It does, of course, relate to all those interests but, fortunately, as the dictionary definition confirms, the word offers wider – and stricter – scope.

The twenty-volume Oxford opines magisterially, but simply, '*Classic: from the Latin classicus: of the highest class, of the first order.*' We thus have fairly high authority for using 'classic' in its strictly lexicographical sense when applied to the gallery of rooms we now parade, for these interiors are certainly classic – that is, of the first order. They are amongst the best of the thousands of rooms recorded on film for *House & Garden* magazine by a group of eminent photographers over the past three or four years and now housed in our archives. Few derive directly from ancient sources, owing little either to the Parthenon or the Pantheon, although the influence of Adam, Soane and other neo-classicists may be detected in numerous instances.

These interiors cannot be classified under such headings as 'period' classics, 'modern' classics or even, most recent of coinages: 'minimalist' classics. A so-called 'classic' chair designed by Corbusier may possibly be featured, but so might a Biedermeier-style table designed and made by an anonymous Swedish or mid-European craftsman. A myriad of influences has gone into making these interiors amongst the best of their kind. The major contribution is, of course, the innate taste of so many gifted amateurs and the contributory flair of professional advisers.

The interiors illustrated in *Classic Rooms* succeed because they demonstrate and evoke that most elusive and covetable of all qualities: a sense of visual delight. Whether we are fortunate enough to have been invited into the rooms or whether we see them only in photographs, we can instantly recognize that the decorative schemes are aesthetically pleasing, interesting and exciting.

These classic rooms reveal that, during the past few years, there has been infinite scope for aesthetic manoeuvre and flair – and change, however subtle. In the 1980s, certain themes and directions in design have been clear to see. Perhaps the most obvious theme is a return to a more traditional, enriched style of decoration, and this is duly reflected in the ten chapters of our book.

Some of the chapters cover specific rooms – dining-rooms, print-rooms and integrated bedrooms-bathrooms – because these have become more significant during the past decade, while other chapters concentrate on current decorative trends, such as the new emphasis on curtain design, the use of mirror, the abundance of stripes, a passion for richer colours, and, most important of all, the rise and rise in general acclaim of the incredibly successful country-house look.

Dining-rooms, above all other rooms, seem to have taken on fresh importance. In the 'sixties and 'seventies there was a notable emphasis on open-plan dining, with the table either in the kitchen-diner or in the living-area. Did this derive from the general sense of social carefreedom evident in novels, plays and films? A few traditionalists may have kept to the more circumspect dining-room, with its grand accoutrements, but they were a minority.

Plus ça change, however: now more people seem to enjoy the experience of entertaining at home in a more sophisticated, though nonetheless relaxed, manner. The dining-room has become a focus for expansive hospitality and a reflection of contemporary life-styles. The style of decoration in the dining-room is often touched by fantasy – from *trompe l'oeil* backgrounds to ornate table settings – but there is an underlying formality, however discreet, which only

Glamorous reflections: *mirrored walls in a sleekly-designed bedroom in Paris (page 60).*

Panelled patinas: *a welcoming hall with wood-grained walls and traditional furniture (page 74).*

Print-rooms revived: *a contemporary setting for a traditional form of decoration (page 100).*

Eccentric spaces: *a circular bedroom in a circular house in Switzerland (page 114).*

Grander windows: *decorative curtains and swags in a London drawing-room (page 138).*

En-suite: *a bathroom marbled and mirrored to match the adjoining bedroom (page 160).*

the most prejudiced of would-be social observers would be likely to deny.

The integrated bedroom-bathroom offers another noticeable change in domestic design. Every new house or flat of any size has at least one bedroom and bathroom *en-suite*, and the bathroom is 'decorated' for pleasure rather than just 'designed' for function. Bathrooms are bigger and more comfortable than ever before, and are often furnished with pictures, rugs, curtains and chairs that echo the decorative theme established in the bedroom. This, too, seems to indicate a shift towards a somewhat more expansive life-style. We lie there soaking in the bath – at least at weekends – and have time to look around. Why not, then, a few paintings, prints, posters to appreciate? Why not a relaxing, upholstered chair for chitter-chat rather than a comfortless, chromium stool?

But of all the current trends in interior decoration, the country-house look has certainly proved to be the most pervasive and persuasive movement of this decade. The look takes many forms and, more often than not, is to be found in the heart of cities, even in converted riverside warehouses and high-rise apartment blocks. A tyro-psychiatrist would probably affirm that such a manner must reflect some kind of yearning to escape from the sharper edges and frenetic pace of modern urban living. No doubt those longings are there in almost every city-dweller, but another explanation may simply be that of all home settings, the traditional country-house interior is the most agreeable, comfortable, reassuring and welcoming.

What other themes in interior decoration have emerged lately? Well, there is clear evidence that curtains have become more elaborate. A decade ago, most windows were hung with simple, straight curtains on plain poles. Now, swags, ropes, tassels, and braids are essential decorative addenda to our curtains. Today's curtain treatments are almost Victorian in their voluptuousness and luxury.

Another touch of decorative nostalgia is the renewed interest in panelling, not necessarily authentic, of course, for much of what appears to be authentic is now pure fake. Thanks to the multi-faceted aspects of the new-old craft of paint-finishing, a seemingly antique patina can be applied to a wall, within a week, and thus give greater decoration and interest to the room. Mirror, too, is now used more frequently, and more boldly, not merely for its unashamed pandering to human vanity, but for its inherent quality of glamour. Indeed, the quest for glamour may well be the key to many of today's preferences in interior design and decoration. Perhaps this derives in part from the glamorous sets seen in films and on television. We want rooms that not only stimulate – and satisfy – our own aesthetic interests and self image, but which also excite the interest of friends and visitors. Hence the revival of richness in decoration. The bland, aseptic and hygienic steeliness of much of yesteryear's modernistic design has clearly given way to this bolder use of colour and pattern and a delighted indulgence in applied decoration.

And, last but not least of our themes are the chapters on print-rooms – a definite, if limited, trend of the late twentieth century – and on rooms of curious shapes. We show the latter because they presented difficult problems for interior decorators yet they all have been dextrously resolved. Their decorative schemes are the best – or shall we say 'classic' – examples of their *genre*.

Although we have concentrated on ten themes in *Classic Rooms*, there are doubtless many other equally decorative themes to be considered at another time. But that, after all, is one of the major pleasures of contemporary interior design: its astonishing and beguiling variety of styles. Take your choice. The truly important theme is to evolve for yourself what is undeniably *your* personal style, which, ultimately, means comfortable, pleasing rooms – and, hopefully, also classics of their kind.

Flexible stripes: *a drawing-room of felicitous lightness and complementary patterns (page 178).*

Dining with panache: *a glistening, theatrical backdrop of marble and silk (page 200).*

Arcadian retreats

Every era produces a characteristic look in interior decoration. The late twentieth century has probably sponsored a greater variety of styles than any previous age but there is one look which, in the light of history, will surely be associated with the nineteen-eighties. That is, the country-house look. Although the look has a long pedigree amongst old-established firms of interior decorators, it has recently been taken up and reworked by a whole host of newcomers, professional and amateur alike. The country-house style has caught the collective imagination. No doubt this is partly a reaction against the dullness of so much modern design, but there are practical reasons, too, for the new-found popularity. The country-house style of furnishing is, above all, comfortable and undemanding. If things get a little out of place, it doesn't matter. An extra bit of clutter on the table; a book or magazine left open on the sofa; squashy cushions; plants . . . these can all be absorbed in the room without destroying the essential harmony and style of the *mise en scène*. The country-house look is friendly and accommodating. You can add to it, change the chair covers, even paste up a wallpaper border, without having to re-do the entire decorative scheme. There is a flexible cosiness about rooms which are furnished in this deceptively unstudied and informal manner.

The extraordinary thing about the country-house style is the enthusiasm with which it has been taken up by people living in towns. Even penthouse flats are given the rural treatment by owners desperate to create the illusion that they are surrounded by fields and trees rather than bricks and mortar. It seems that we are all searching for a domestic arcadia.

One of the most obviously arcadian settings illustrated here is the drawing-room on page 38. This is a masterly equation of formality and informality. The arrangement of the furniture and pictures is symmetrical and balanced, yet the overall impression is pleasingly untrammeled. This free, unlaboured trait is fundamental in achieving the authentic country-house look. Too many plain surfaces and carefully-matched fabrics and wallpapers are to be avoided. So, too, are strident colours. The successful country-house interior combines lots of patterns and varied seating, seemingly the product of the tastes and purchases of several generations. It has evolved slowly, almost imperceptively, over a period of time, rather than been put together in an instant. The room has a sense of permanence and reassurance.

The octagonal morning-room at Sudeley Castle in Gloucestershire, decorated by Lady Ashcombe with Colefax & Fowler, encapsulates the English country-house interior. Assured informality and comfort are based on traditional furniture and lots of patterns. The stencilled walls follow a Tudor rose theme.

TIMELESS INVOCATIONS

Two of the many pleasures invoked in a well considered room in the country are a feeling of timeless comfort and an awareness of the garden. Both pleasures can be experienced in this Oxfordshire drawing-room decorated by Nessa O'Neill with Gabriele Langer of Beaudesert. The satisfying timelessness and gardenesque ambience have been achieved by the judicious use of tranquil, reassuring colours; lots of flowers, real and printed; and commodious seating piled with cushions.

RURAL ILLUSION

Although the monumental stone chimneypiece suggests a room deep in the countryside, this setting by Nina Campbell is in the heart of London. The rural illusion is enhanced by the informal mix of furniture and patterns, by the wood carving on the chimneybreast, the leather screen and Gothic oak table.

Even the paintings, particularly the large eighteenth-century oil of a family group by Van der Helft, allude to the country-house style of decoration. One of the most notable elements in the room is the magnificent Mosulipatan rug which inspired the entire colour-scheme.

A PERVASIVE EASE

Though possessed of architectural grandeur, this drawing-room in a fine neo-classical mansion is very much a family room where ease and naturalness are all-important. The room conveys the much sought-after quality of having evolved artlessly and gradually rather than having been designed instantly on a drawing-board. No two chairs or sofas seem to match, yet there is a pervasive harmony. Yellow-ochre walls, painted to simulate fabric, are offset by chintz, and the doors are tortoiseshelled. The house was decorated with advice from Prue Lane Fox.

SUBTLE PATTERNING

England can claim no monopoly in the English country-house style of decoration. Here, the authentic look has been achieved in a villa in Switzerland – admittedly, with advice from an English decorator, Tom Parr of Colefax & Fowler. A characteristic feature is the arrangement of furniture in informal groups, creating several seating-areas, each semi-independent but sufficiently open to link across to one another. Another characteristic to note is the lack of plain surfaces and fabrics. Everything is patterned, however subtly, thus avoiding a contrived, matched dullness.

SIMPLE SOPHISTICATION

An 1820s Gothic lodge in the
Cotswolds is the setting for
this decoratively Gothicised
sitting-room by George
Cooper. Though distinctly
countrified in spirit, the

room is decorated with
sophisticated lightness rather
than clumsy rusticity. There
is a pleasing simplicity in the
stone chimneypiece and
coconut matting, but the

painted armchairs and *fauteuil* lend refinement and poise. The 'bookcases' at the far end are, in fact, painted cupboard doors concealing heating units and stereo equipment. Many of the books have witty titles, all part of David Mendl's skilful brushwork. The walls are rag-rolled in a creamy shade of buttermilk, with cornice and skirting brought out in a darker beige. The curtains and long cloth are of cream silk with contrasting edgings and generous fringe.

A FELICITOUS MEDLEY

Cosiness and controlled clutter create an inviting, country identity in this first-floor drawing-room in a town house in London. The felicitous medley of period furniture, textiles and decorative objects was assembled by Jilly Kelly and put together with skilful freedom. Above the Victorian sofa, with its original heavy fringe, is a series of antique watercolours of flowers and fruit. The arrangement is symmetrical but the different sizes and frames ensure that the effect is neither rigid nor obvious. Indeed, there is very little that is obvious about this room. It is a highly individual interpretation of the country-house look, with walls 'aged' with a 'cobweb' wash and woodwork subtly grained by paint specialist Jez Etheridge.

SPACE FOR LINGERING

An enviable attribute of the ideal country house is a spacious, welcoming hall. When interior designer Anthony Sykes refurbished a turn-of-the-century house less than half-a-dozen miles from Hyde Park Corner, he removed the wall between the front sitting-room and narrow passageway in order to attain a large, characteristically rural entrance. The walls of the hall are hung with family portraits; furniture is a mixture of polished oak and painted wood; bookcases flank the open fireplace. In such a countrified environment, it is easy to imagine green fields outside. Unlike most urban halls, this is an interesting, enjoyable space in which to linger.

PATTERNED UNITY

In spite of multitudinous patterns, this drawing-room in London is suffused with a serene unity. The key to the seeming contradiction is the magnificent Agra carpet. This inspired the colours of the walls – a subtle paint finish in sea-foam green – and of the curtains which, together, make a restful and pleasing balance. The green is also a particularly good backdrop for the group portrait by Howard Morgan above the sofa. All the colours of the textiles, old and new, are gentle and undemanding. In a room seeking to establish the country-house look, such quietude is *de rigueur*. This room was decorated with advice from Antonv Ormiston.

HISTORICAL ROMANCE

Any room with the unmistakable stamp of history is romantic. With its ancient stone walls, carved stone fireplace and ribbed ceiling, this grand drawing-room in Sudeley Castle, the Gloucestershire home of Lord and Lady Ashcombe, is no exception. The setting is remindful of a chequered and eventful past – Sudeley dates back many centuries and was the Royalist headquarters during the Civil War – but the present scheme for the furnishing of the private rooms, devised by Lady Ashcombe in conjunction with Colefax & Fowler, makes elegant concessions to contemporary comfort and country-house furnishing. In keeping with the robust architecture, the furniture, whether antique or modern, is substantial in size and vigorous in style. The flamboyantly carved and gilded side-table beneath the Van Dyke portrait is particularly handsome.

QUINTESSENTIAL GEORGIAN

Built in 1750, Easton Grey in Wiltshire, the home of Didi Saunders, is the quintessential Georgian country house. The restrained grandeur of the entrance-hall is established by fine proportions rather than by elaborate decoration. The floor is left bare, but a pair of tapestries hung against the terracotta-coloured walls has a mellowing influence. Most of the furniture and decorative objects are arranged in pairs, the symmetry making an important contribution to the room's understated formality and elegance.

RECURRING THEMES

Flowers, especially roses, are recurring themes in this oblong drawing-room with unusual chintz-covered 'back-to-back' sofa. The impression given by the informal grouping of comfortable, mixed seating is friendly and unconstrained. Curtains of cream grosgrain are edged with the same chintz as the sofa and stool.

A BOOKISH RETREAT

Traditionally, every country house of any importance had a library of aesthetic as well as intellectual interest. The tradition is ably maintained in this contemporary example in Pennsylvania decorated by Thomas Kyle and Jerome Murray. Like all the best libraries, it is supremely comfortable and invites reading. The arrangement of the furniture and the focus of the decoration are cosy and inward-looking. There are myriad things to appeal to the eye and mind – including the paintings which are hung unconventionally, but highly effectively, against the bookshelves.

VIRTUOSO COMPOSITION

Decorated by Tom Parr of Colefax & Fowler, the drawing-room at Easton Grey House in Wiltshire – see, too, pages 30–31 – is a virtuoso composition in blue and white, warmed by touches of colour in the chintz. Even the floor has been stencilled with blue flowers on a white background. While lending an appropriately light, country look to the room, the stencilling, by Jim Smart, has the practical advantage of disguising the indifferent wood of the floorboards. The shade of blue used on the walls is an especially responsive background for the series of black-and-white engravings depicting views of Rome.

A DELICATE BALANCE

Few drawing-rooms manage to equate formality and informality, but this room, designed by Prue Lane Fox, in a classical 1840s house, displays both qualities in equal quantities. This is not a room of stifling exactness, but neither is it unstructured. Everything is very carefully considered, both from the point of view of colour and disposition of objects. The 'weights' of the greens, pinks and blues are well matched, while the pictures and console tables are placed symmetrically. Occasional tables with pots of flowers break up the space; the exaggerated dragged paint finish on the walls is a deft background for varied pictures and textiles.

Gorgeous colour

The decoration of a room can undoubtedly influence the mood of its occupants. We all know instinctively that certain colours induce calm while others generate excitement. And we all recognize that there are some combinations of colours which, quite literally, are nauseating. Perhaps this is why there is a temptation to play safe with colour and to use bland shades in obvious juxtapositions. What a pity! There are so many brilliant possibilities afforded by strong, positive colours that we shouldn't allow ourselves to be intimidated. We should experiment with colour, flaunt it, use it with confidence and zest.

The rooms in this chapter all display confidence and bravura. They are bold, resolute rooms where intense, solid colour is the dominant theme. Red seems to be the favourite – probably because it is such a resoundingly successful background in cool climates, especially in rooms furnished with decorative antiques – but it is by no means the only choice. Imperial blue, emerald green and dazzling yellow are all used with verve and conviction.

One of the most noticeable aspects of today's strongly coloured paintwork is its texture and finish. Plain paint has been ousted by dragged, stippled, sponged, rag-rolled, marbled and other decorative effects. These are invariably an improvement on vast planes of bright, flat paintwork – the sort of thing that was fashionable in the 'sixties – because the finish is softer and more sympathetic to the traditional styles of furniture which are now so much in vogue. But not all the rooms illustrated here use paint to achieve their vivid colouring. In some instances, the wall finish is fabric which, again, has a softer, more sensual appearance and looks well with antique furniture and paintings.

The use of big, bright colours take assurance and dash, but it makes an impact that can rarely be achieved by other means. Take Nancy Young's vivid green room on page 48 and try to imagine the same space painted magnolia. You don't have to be a clairvoyant to know that the room wouldn't have a fraction of the panache seen here. Panache is also evident in the deep-blue room on page 44, where black is added for even greater drama. This is a strong, sophisticated scheme with no-nonsense patterns, no frills and no fussy detailing. The uncompromising colour is well matched by the disciplined furnishing.

Brilliant coral-red walls and limed-wood dado are complemented by coral-and-white curtains in a dining-room decorated by Sisi Edmiston. The ebullient colour-scheme and double-looped curtains deliberately emphasize the room's height. The pale cloth and chair-covers accentuate the red.

ECHOES OF PROUST

Aesthetic considerations are all too often sacrificed – or, at least, compromised – for comfort, but this room, designed by Brian Juhos, is a visual triumph as well as cossetting home. He has used period furnishings – mainly late-eighteenth- and early-nineteenth-century – in an ample manner, recalling the fullness and luxe of *fin de siècle* Proustian interiors. The red mullion twill on the walls is a gloriously rich, dramatic background for the assembly of paintings, porcelain, gilt and dark-wood furniture.

GRAPHIC PARTNERSHIP

In a sitting-room designed by Bill Bennette, the combination of deep blue and black makes a graphic background for contemporary pictures, Pre-Columbian artefacts and African Gold Coast masks. Skilful lighting focuses on the primitive forms and reinforces the room's bold, theatrical ambience. To counteract the forcefulness of the blue, the wall finish is a soft-textured bouclé velvet, while fine black, slatted blinds and tailored seating are well suited to the room's clean, unfussy arrangement.

A DISCERNING CONFIDENCE

Henri Samuel is one of France's – if not the world's – most renowned decorators whose reputation has been established over many decades. His own home, in the Faubourg St Honoré in Paris, reflects his original and discerning eye which has never become fixed in a particular period or style. He hangs his remarkable collection of modern pictures – including Balthus' 'Strawberries' above the chimneypiece – against walls lined with Pompeiian-red fabric. The colour, tinged with russet, is an admirable foil for twentieth-century canvases as well as for varied furniture, some antique, some of our own time. The room is a strong statement of well-informed eclecticism and confident taste.

AN UNEQUIVOCAL ENVIRONMENT

Few design schemes in a nineteenth-century flat in London could be more fearless and exhilarating than this vast, green-and-black living-area devised by Nancy Young. The walls, lacquered by Graham Carr, provide a high-spirited, highly individual environment for a collection of mirrored and chromed Art Deco furniture intermingled with antiques. The unequivocal treatment of the parquet floor uses green and black staining to create ziggurat bands extending the full length of the room.

A CONGENIAL BACKGROUND

Flat paint in a strong colour is rarely successful as a wall finish in a traditional drawing-room – hence the choice, here, of a sophisticated, mottled effect, carried out by Mark and Rosie Hornak. The specialist finish makes a refined and congenial background for pictures ranging from costume and stage designs to nineteenth-century views of London. The pale dado – marbled to match the chimneypiece – and curtains intensify the impact of the red. Gothic bookcases, chairs and cornice are light contributions, both in colour and form, to the room's spontaneous and cheerful personality. The scheme was carried out with advice from George Cooper of Cooper & Perkins.

SHADES OF EMPIRE

A dark blue glaze guarantees an appropriately Imperial background for a French Empire bed with ormolu mounts and resplendent hangings. The blue is contrasted with a powerful shade of golden-yellow, equally appropriate for the style and period of the furniture. Next to the window is a splendid cupboard with fabric-lined glazed doors. This distinctly masculine dressing-room was designed by Rosemary Hamilton.

PLEASING INTENSITY

Although this room uses a lot of intense colour, the general impression is not heavy, due largely to the particular shade of red and to the gentle glow of the paint finish. The adroit finish was achieved by applying four coats of paint and varnish. First, the walls were loosely dragged with colour; then a wash was applied; finally came two coats of matt varnish. The pale ceiling and dado offset the red, while the chintz curtains identify with both areas of colour and correlate the variety of upholstery fabrics. The room was designed with assistance from Sophia Stainton.

THE COLOUR OF SUNLIGHT

Brilliant yellow, like an all-enveloping shaft of sunlight, coats this sitting-room in London, designed by Diana Griffin-Strauss for Henry and Jane Carlton. The stippled finish on the walls, carried out by Leo Seymour, softens the intensity of the colour without lessening its impact. The same yellow is seen in different guises in the patterned upholstery and cushions and in the fringed edging to the pelmets. Altogether, the room has an enlivening joyfulness which is especially enticing in an inner-city setting.

RESOLUTELY RED

The owners of this drawing-room, decorated by Cynthia Clarry, have an extensive collection of traditional pictures, including black-and-white engravings and colourful oils. To some extent, the pictures dictated the choice of wall treatment. Cynthia Clarry decided on fabric as this not only gives a degree of luxury but is an excellent background for pictures of all sorts. The deep red of the fabric is balanced by the green carpet. The combination is resolute and rich, while the pattern of the chintz incorporates both colours and is dense enough to hold its own within the overall scheme. Note the brass hooks used to hang the engravings: an unusual touch which discreetly breaks up the rigid rows.

Glamorous reflections

Mirror is one of the most effective tools available to the interior decorator. It can make small rooms seem larger; dark rooms seem lighter; mundane rooms more glamorous. Glamour is what mirror is all about. Even a small looking-glass above a chimneypiece can enliven a room, but panels of wall-mirror, strategically placed, are best of all devices to lift a room out of the ordinary. Mirror also has the advantage of looking compatible in traditional and modern settings, affiliating as well with important antiques as with bare floorboards. The rooms at right and on page 70 demonstrate the ability of mirror to integrate in widely differing settings.

One of the subtlest but most effective ways of using mirror is to line the wall with it between a pair of windows, as seen on page 67. Although the mirror is used in a limited quantity, it produces a feeling of great lightness, deceiving the eye into thinking that the whole wall is glazed.

A curious, almost surreal effect is created when pictures are hung against mirror. When you enter the room shown on page 68, you have the impression that the prints are floating in mid air. What is supporting the pictures? Is there a wall or isn't there? In fact, this room shows a brilliant use of mirror in every way. The space is tiny yet the effect is grand and distinguished. It is impossible to believe that the seating-area is only nine feet square because the style of decoration makes few concessions to scaling-down, and the mirror, which clads the entire wall opposite the windows, redoubles the light and space.

Another room which uses mirror on a lavish scale is the dining-room on page 62. This room is comparatively thinly furnished, giving a good feeling of openness, which is further enhanced by the wall of reflective glass. The dining-room opens into a music-room which, in turn, opens into a drawing-room. The fireplace wall in the latter area is also mirrored, so the boundaries of the tripartite enfilade are blurred and diffuse. At night, wall sconces fixed to the mirror give countless reflections and glitter.

French interior decoration has a well-established tradition of using mirror. Two highly sophisticated examples of current schemes, both in Paris, are shown on pages 64 and 72.

In the suavely-decorated bedroom of his Second Empire flat in Paris, designer Claude Vicario de la Iglesia has lined the walls with free-falling fabric and mirror. The fabric is looped back, curtain-like, over the mirror behind the chest-of-drawers, while a handsome, Louis XV provincial armoire is reflected in the mirror behind the bed.

MIRRORED ENFILADE

This dining-room, designed by Elizabeth Cranmer, is part of an enfilade opening into a music-room, thence into a drawing-room. The wide archways between the rooms give a generous sense of space, enhanced by the use of mirror. In the drawing-room, seen at the far end in the smaller photograph, the entire chimneypiece wall is faced with 'antique' mirror-glass, while, in the dining-room, the chimneypiece wall is clad with plain mirror. In both rooms, wall sconces are superimposed on the mirror, giving, at night, additional sparkle and reflections. The magnificent tapestry came from France, as did the late-eighteenth-century basket-weave chairs.

SUSPENDED IN SPACE

Designer Claude Vicario de la Iglesia is an eclectic who never hesitates to mix modern and antique furniture and to display objects from different cultures. His interiors are always notable for unexpected and original touches. Note the outsize pots and the narrow band of chintz on the curtains which cross-refers to the upholstery and cushions. Note, too, the placing of the painting and pair of pots on gilt brackets against the wall of mirror, giving the curious impression that they are suspended in space.

SUBTLE BUT EFFECTIVE

Mirror need not be deployed in an obvious manner to be effective. Here, in a double drawing-room designed by Mimmi O'Connell for Nadia and Michael Goedhuis, tall, narrow panels of mirror have been used subtly to line the areas of wall between, and adjacent to, the windows. Because the mirror is seen in conjunction with the vistas through the windows, it doubly confuses the eye, suggesting that the walls are entirely glazed. Another large panel of mirror is used above the chimneypiece. This, too, increases the sensation of light and space, reflecting the burnt siena tones of the wall finish and Michael Goedhuis' fine collection of post-classical Chinese and Japanese bronzes.

SPARKLING IMAGES

This room is minuscule yet successfully combines a comfortable seating-area, dining-area and kitchen. The seating-area measures a mere nine feet square but there is no compromise about scaling down the furniture or using mundane decoration. Instead, designer Brian Juhos has made a bold choice of good, traditional pieces with pleasing proportions. There is no hint of claustrophobia in the room, thanks to the integrated, restful colour-scheme and the lavish installation of mirror opposite the windows. In spite of its diminutive size and open-plan arrangement, this interior has real glamour.

ART AND NATURE

Kenneth Turner is celebrated for his unique flower sculptures, but he is also a designer of settings for glittering parties and, as seen here, of rooms with a pleasingly natural, uncalculated style of decoration. To achieve such an unaffected look takes care and sensitivity. Kenneth Turner is a passionate gardener who believes that indoors and outdoors should be closely related – hence the many plants that flourish in this sitting-room. But his love of nature is matched by a keen appreciation of man-made artefacts and artifice. Antique busts and furniture are juxtaposed with plain floorboards; a classical bronze figure stands beside a humble wooden bowl. These juxtapositions are reflected in the mirrored recesses to either side of the chimneybreast, where the glass creates areas of lustre and 'polish'.

DUAL PURPOSE

The dual roles of this room in Paris are reflected extremely decoratively in the mirror-glass which lines the wall behind the sideboard and glazes the small-pane double doors. (The latter, incidentally, were added purely to balance the design of the room and serve no other

purpose.) Not wishing to give over a room solely to eating, Claude Vicario de la Iglesia decided to combine it with a library. The combination works well from a practical viewpoint and, aesthetically, the books help to overcome that feeling of bleakness which sometimes pervades dining-rooms. The juxtaposition of cornflower-blue walls with white woodwork and ceiling is fresh and dynamic.

Panelled patinas

A few years ago, panelling was so unfashionable that even unique, early examples were stripped out and burnt. Now, people living in old, once-panelled houses have a deeper appreciation of the appropriateness of this wall finish and are seeking to re-install it, restore it and, if necessary, fake it. Even rooms which were never panelled in the past are being given this treatment – a measure of the prevailing wish to be surrounded by historical allusions and to establish a framework of domestic cosiness.

The rooms in this chapter show panelling of all sorts, ranging from polished oak to simulated marble. The most authentic versions are solid wood, but others are the results of ingenious *trompe l'oeil* paintwork. The sitting-room shown on page 80, for example, looks for all the world as though it is panelled with marble. In fact, it is nothing of the sort – just ordinary plaster brilliantly painted to simulate four different stones. Traditionally, panelling is composed of solid planes of cladding, but an alternative effect can be achieved with applied mouldings, as in Emanuelle Khanh's flat in Paris, shown on page 94, and in Michael Reeves' converted ballroom in London (page 82). In the latter, the mouldings are superbly elaborate. In both rooms, colour is minimal and the panelling is seen at its most effective.

If you are using applied mouldings to create panels, the important thing to remember is that the panelling should correspond to the room's architecture. Panelling is an excellent way to break up large areas of blank wall, but the panels need to be of the right proportions if they are to look comfortable. And, if you intend to hang pictures on a panelled wall, it is essential to take into account their shape and size. Well-considered panelling is an effective means of 'framing' paintings, giving additional interest to their presentation, but if the relationship between the pictures and mouldings is wrong, then the effect is disastrous.

One of the most decoratively panelled rooms illustrated here is the dining-room on page 96. The walls are set out with rectangles stencilled in the eighteenth-century Swedish manner, giving a light, charming character echoed by the painted chairs.

The panelled walls of this archetypal country hall in a Queen Anne hunting-lodge were previously dark and gloomy. Now painted by Nemone Burgess to simulate ash, the honey-toned panelling has given the hall an altogether more welcoming atmosphere and off-sets the darker woods of the furniture.

GRAND BUT UNPRETENTIOUS

During the past two centuries, this room in a house in Brussels has seen many changes. At the time of the Battle of Waterloo, the house was the French embassy, and during the Second World war it was used as offices. Latterly, it took on a more peaceful and domestic role when it became the family home of Bernard and Laura Ashley. The Ashleys restored the interior in keeping with the period of the building, but the style of furnishing, while totally sympathetic to the building, displays a pleasing informality well suited to a family home. This panelled library, with its contrast-painted mouldings and pilasters, is typical of the late Laura Ashley's ability to cope with a grand room in an unpretentious and charming manner. The seating, relaxed in style and arrangement, looks comfortable and inviting around the imposing grey marble chimneypiece. Portraits, including one of Augusta, Princess of Wales, are suspended from cheerful bows. Patterns are mixed and unstudied. (The yellow panelled drawing-room of the same house is shown on pages 92–93.)

PANELLED PARADOX

This panelled room in an early eighteenth-century house in an English country town is a striking example of a formal yet unintimidating style of decoration. The key to the paradox is the all-enveloping warmth derived from rich textures and colours. The deep tones of the oak-lined walls and wood furniture are a splendid foil for sumptuous fabrics used for upholstery and curtains. The latter are of night-blue silk, while the sofa is covered in deep pink moiré. The French provincial wing chairs are covered in a patterned fabric which combines the main colours seen in the room. The rugs, too, combine reds and blues and are appropriately weighty in tone and pattern for such a masculine setting. The vitrines were specially made in old oak to integrate with the walls. In addition to their display function, the cabinets house drinks and a stereo unit. The room was decorated by Rosemary Hamilton.

DIVERTING ATTENTION

Marbled walls in antique colours evoke Pompeii in a sitting-room decorated by Mimmi O'Connell. The strong architectural treatment diverts attention from the room's awkward shape and asymmetrically positioned windows. An equally strong line has been taken in the choice of textiles, which include striped cottons, damasks and plain silks. The curtaining is an unusual combination of Austrian blinds and single dress curtains held back with cords and tassels. The poles are Regency-style arrows in black and gilt. The illusionistic paintwork was carried out by Peter Farlow.

WITHIN A BALLROOM

Michael Reeves is a fashion designer, an interior designer and an antique dealer. These tripartite interests are all reflected in the distinctive decoration of his flat in London. When he bought the flat, it comprised four bed-sits, but to his surprise and pleasure he subsequently discovered that the insubstantial partition walls were built within a nineteenth-century ballroom with mouldings and mirrors virtually all intact. After removing the subdivisions,

Michael Reeves had a fantastic space for a bright airy drawing-room with galleries housing the kitchen, dining-room and bedroom. He restored·the original panelled plasterwork on the walls and painted the room the palest taupe, a restful background for a mixture of old and new furniture, much of which is positioned, unusually, on the diagonal. The imposing wooden chimneypiece was designed by Michael Reeves to replace the original piece which had been removed.

PAINTED FRAMEWORK

Pale mouldings applied to coral-stippled walls create a panelled framework for Lord and Lady Wilton's fine collection of paintings. Animal subjects are a favourite theme: a pair of sporting oils by Wootton flanks the chimneypiece on which stands a German china elephant; a cut-out of the family border terrier stands in front of the fire; a pair of Chinese pottery ducks sits atop the tall chest. When the Wiltons moved into the flat, the curtains were already *in situ*. On the advice of Tom Parr of Colefax & Fowler, they retained the curtains but added a deep bullion fringe. An armchair and sofa were covered in the same printed fabric, while another sofa and armchair were upholstered in a taupe-coloured linen piped in coral. Decorative cushions in old and new fabrics introduce toning colours and a variety of different textures.

CELESTIAL BLUE

In a William and Mary manor-house decorated by George Spencer of Sloane Street, the main bedroom is a summery chorus of blue and white. The frieze above the wall panelling is picked out in white against a blue background, as is the decorative detailing on the Louis XVI-style bed. The white chintz bedcover is quilted with blue thread and finished with blue-and-white fan edging. The sofa and chairs are piled with the owner's collection of cushions in every size and shape, mainly covered in white cotton and lace. The white carpet, printed cotton curtains and frilled dressing-table skirt contribute to the room's delicacy and femininity.

BENEATH A SUMMER SKY

This dining-room in a mid-nineteenth-century house in France, restored and redecorated by Victoire and Patrick de Montal, is full of originality and surprise: behind the subtly-painted panelling is a series of capacious cupboards; the ceiling is a gentle evocation of a summer sky; the painted chairs are of different styles but share a degree of lightness without seeming flimsy. The blue of the chair covers is picked up by the curtains and tablecloth and by the silk covering for the chandelier chain. The chandelier, candelabra, clock and mirror are flamboyant elements in a room which has that unique, timeless quality inherent in French country mansions.

GOLDEN INSPIRATION

When Sisi Edmiston took over this sitting-room in a house in London, the panelling was badly damaged. Wherever possible, it was repaired, but elsewhere mouldings have been replaced and skilfully integrated by Sarah Shearer's paintwork. The old-gold colour-scheme of the room was inspired by the magnificent four-panelled Flemish screen mounted on the wall opposite the chimneypiece. The curtains are generously gathered and held back at high level in order to reveal the elegant window arches and to allow the shutters to open and close.

DOUBLE SPACE

Vivid yellow moiré fabric, tempered by clear-grey paintwork, makes a striking effect in the panelled drawing-room of an eighteenth-century house in Brussels restored and decorated by Bernard and Laura Ashley. (See, too, pages 76–77.) This double room, divided by a columned arch, comprises a relaxed seating-area with cushioned sofas grouped round a low table, and a more 'upright' area with a full-height, circular table and a set of French chairs. The curtains at both ends of the room have simple headings embellished by a delicate arrangement of rope and tassels. The two parts of the room have similar rugs forming an additional link.

CLASSIC CHIC

Dress designer Emmanuelle Khanh's flat in Paris exudes relaxed confidence and classic chic. She chose the flat in a typical 1880s building on the Left Bank because she liked the large rooms and tall windows. The panelled walls are painted white and the furniture is kept to a minimum in order not to lose the sense of space and light. As it happens, the emphatic shapes of the well-chosen pieces of Art Deco benefit from being surrounded by plenty of air. The windows, too, are airily treated with sheer curtains instead of heavy drapes. Most of the decorative objects are placed at low level, but there is much visual interest higher up derived from the bold plasterwork.

TRANSATLANTIC INFLUENCES

If you detect an American influence in this London dining-room, it is probably because its designer, Sandra Coxe of Coxe Designs, comes from the East Coast of America, and, furthermore, she conferred on the project with New York decorator, Ann LeConey. But there are European influences, too: the walls have been painted with *trompe l'oeil* panelling by Graham Carr in a style and colours that are typically eighteenth-century Swedish. The painted chairs also have a Continental flavour. The table, however, is American, an eighteenth-century design by Duncan Phyfe, and the fabric for the curtains is American. Although the entire bay is curtained, the side window have mirrored shutters. These were installed to rectify the bay's ungainly proportions.

PANELS WITHIN PANELS

Panelling, dragged and stippled in two shades of green, frames a series of French painted panels depicting figures and flowers in rococo cartouches. The greens are repeated in the upholstery of the seating, which comprises alternating sets of Regency and high-backed contemporary chairs. This boldly executed, unusual scheme was devised by Dale Tryon.

Print-rooms revived

When pasted directly on to walls and outlined with decorative paper borders, even the most serious of engravings can generate a pleasing lightness – and lightheartedness – rarely achieved when prints are framed behind glass. Print-rooms combine a sense of history and culture with a touch of frivolity and unpredictability which, nowadays, when so many rooms are decorated to a formula, is unusually appealing. Indeed, few themes in interior decoration are as satisfying to the eye and mind as an assured print-room.

The first print-rooms were made in the mid-eighteenth century. Throughout the next fifty or so years, many such rooms were set out, some of the finest being at Stratfield Saye in Hampshire. At one time, that house – which later became the home of the 1st Duke of Wellington – had nine print-rooms, several of which survive to this day, including a particularly handsome gallery with gold-leaf decoration. A few houses owned by the National Trust, including Blickling Hall in Norfolk and The Vyne in Hampshire, also have print-rooms open to the public. Now that this charming form of decoration is enjoying a revival, these historical examples are excellent sources of reference.

Choosing a background colour for the walls in a print-room is not as difficult as one might think. Vivid backgrounds cast black-and-white engravings into bold relief; bland backgrounds allow the prints to speak for themselves. Curiously, many recently-made print-rooms are also dining-rooms. Red is a well-proven background for dining and, coincidentally, looks well with black-and-white engravings.

Even more important than the background colour is the setting-out of the prints and the use of borders and other printed embellishments. Generally, prints should be set out in symmetrical compositions, closely related to the scale and shapes of the walls on to which they are pasted. To achieve a balanced, harmonious effect will prove difficult if the engravings are considered individually rather than as groups. Black-and-white line engravings of architectural subjects and classical statues are ideal for print-rooms as they have such clear definition, but coloured prints can also work, though the choice of background wall colour needs rather more care and consideration.

Happily, creating an authentic effect in a print-room need cost very little. The prints and borders can be modern copies – or even photocopies – providing the quality of the paper looks right.

The theme of this print-room in the Berkeley Hotel, London, designed by Prue Lane Fox, is based on the life of the 1st Duke of Wellington – an appropriate subject as he himself had several print-rooms at his home at Stratfield Saye. The room shown here was executed by Nicola Wingate-Saul and Pierre Spake.

CONFIDENT USE OF COLOUR

There is nothing half-hearted about this dining-room in which the confident use of Pompeiian red, generously juxtaposed with white, makes a dramatic impact. The scheme is disciplined, both in the limited palette and symmetrical grouping of prints, yet there is a sense of vitality, thanks to the strong colour and variety of print subjects. The large room, in a nineteenth-century house in London, is semi-divided by a depressed archway, the latter echoed by a mirrored alcove in which stands a carved wood sideboard. The dining-table is covered with a plain white cloth, an unbeatable underpinning for classic china and glass, and particularly suitable in a traditional setting.

RESTFUL AND RESTRAINED

This bedroom, with prints supplied and arranged by Nicola Wingate-Saul, is something of a paradox. At first glance, it seems very simple: the colours are undemanding, there is comparatively little pattern, and the style of furniture is restrained. Yet, when one considers the room more carefully, that first impression proves deceptive. To combine a romantic frieze of swagged flowers with classical prints could be a disaster but, here, the effect is one of harmony and appropriateness, realized by some skilful cross-references. The frieze refers to the swagged mouldings on the chimneypiece; the pair of figures on the mantelshelf answers those in the engravings; the *trompe l'oeil* panels beneath the printed dado rail reflect the panelling of the door.

AGAINST AN IVORY BACKGROUND

In this ivory-coloured dining-room in a Georgian house in London, intricate borders and sinuous ropes ensure that the eighteenth-century prints have appealing gaiety in spite of the classical sobriety of some of the elevations and plans. The engravings were supplied and set out by Pierre Spake and Nicola Wingate-Saul, who also produced the paper frieze, ropes and mouldings. The open fire and bookshelves contribute a library-like ambience, reinforced by neo-classical chairs and deep blue curtains. Between this and the adjoining room are oak double doors with burr fields and ebonized mouldings, designed by Anthony Paine. The room has sense of tradition yet is totally unstuffy.

INSPIRATION FOR TODAY

Many print-rooms were created in the late eighteenth and early nineteenth centuries but none is more strikingly elegant than this lake-green example in Rosersberg, one of Sweden's most notable royal palaces. The room has numerous elements to inspire a print-room for today: clear colours, a painted floor and neo-classical decorative objects. The clarity of the green, enhanced by gold and white woodwork and mouldings, ensures that the subtle tones of the hand-coloured prints are not overpowered by the force of the wall colour. The prints, bought by Carl XIII during visits to Germany and Switzerland, depict a diversity of subjects unified by consistent borders and rigid setting-out. The floor is decorated with octagons and lozenges simulating stone.

A CONVIVIAL MEETING-ROOM

Recently redecorated under the direction of Anthony Marsh and Colin Mackay, the dining-room at Sotheby's doubles as the boardroom. Unlike most corporate meeting-rooms, which tend to be rather sterile, this room is pleasingly intimate and decorative. The print-room theme is unusual enough to prompt lively conversation amongst guests at lunch, while the colour of the walls is a suitably recessive background for business conferences. The subtlety of the finish was achieved by using book cloth to which a green glaze has been applied for greater depth and texture.

The prints, representing the *Monuments in the Gardens of Versailles* by Le Pautre, were engraved during the latter half of the seventeenth century but the borders are new. The dado panels and simulated stone chimneypiece were skilfuly painted by Geoffrey Lamb and Michael Daly.

BOTANICAL THEMES

Most print-rooms use black-and-white engravings but this small bathroom, decorated by Jane Churchill, is prettily decked out with coloured engravings. The new borders, printed in black on white paper, have been colour-washed to link in with the antique prints. The walls are stippled in a soft pink, a flattering background for the botanical pictures and, at the same time, a hospitable colour for a room which, too often, can seem cold and comfortless. Pink is also a pleasing foil for the dark-wood cupboards. Mirror on both sides of the narrow room increases the illusion of space and multiplies the prints *ad infinitum*.

Eccentric spaces

Rooms with unusual architectural features are invariably appealing. Sometimes the appeal is purely visual, but often the fascination derives from an historical, associative element which arouses our curiosity and appeals to our intellect. Ancient timbers, Gothic windows, a viewing gallery . . . these romantic reminders of a building's former life prompt enjoyable speculation on past events and inhabitants.

The rooms shown in this chapter are all architectural curiosities. None is a straightforward, modern rectangle. Some are conversions of strange, unlikely buildings, whether a *bergerie* in France, a granary in Wiltshire or a billiards room in London. Others are attic spaces with sloping walls and low ceilings, or studio rooms with great height. Yet others are round or oval, have massive beams or soaring windows. The one thing all these rooms have in common is that they challenge the skills of the interior decorator and, in every case, their decoration has been successfuly handled with originality and flair.

The most striking example of a decoration scheme which complements the unusual architecture is, paradoxically, the most understated: the finishes and furnishing of the circular, domed bedroom shown at right maximise the room's form by avoiding the distractions of colour and by placing the bed in the centre of the floor beneath a draped hoop. The result is like an ethereal, classical temple. In contrast, the yellow drawing-room on page 126 uses bold colour specifically to emphasize the architecture by drawing the eye right up to the ridge of the open ceiling.

The white bedroom and yellow drawing-room are very different in character but both are in old buildings. It is a sad indictment of today's architecture that it is easier to find architectural interest in old structures than it is in new ones. Happily, though, there are exceptions, such as the drawing-room on page 132. This room is a new extension to a period house in Gloucestershire but it has masses of style and interest. Not only do the Gothic windows copy the shape of the windows in the original building, but the room's overall form, with its semi-open roof and applied mouldings, is spectacularly well composed.

In order not to detract from its classical, temple-like form and fine architectural detailing, this circular bedroom in a circular house in Switzerland – see, too, pages 130–131 – is decorated and furnished exclusively in palest ivory-white. Behind the columns, a painted panorama of an idyllic landscape recedes into the distance.

IN AN ERSTWHILE BARN

An old Wiltshire barn, dismantled and moved to a different site on the same estate, now forms an unique drawing-room attached to an early seventeenth-century house. With pale grey walls, graduated blue ceiling and casually draped seating, the room has a vivifying lightness and informality. The seating covers are Indian shawls, while the curtains are of checked shantung. The main doors, originally from a fifteenth-century Spanish chapel, inspired the detail of the bookcases to either side.

UNDER THE EAVES

Jo Robinson, the owner-decorator of this sitting-room in Kensington, has courage and panache. Far from being intimidated by the modest, attic-like feel of the architecture and by the off-centre chimneypiece, she has furnished the room with exuberant patterns and has emphasized the eccentricity of the fireplace by grouping a series of silhouettes on one side only. The curtain treatment also shows panache. As the slope of the window wall ruled out long curtains, the simplest solution would have been to hang straight, sill-length curtains – but how dull they would have been compared with this elegant, pull-up arrangement in rich blue silk!

ROMANTIC FRANCE

Few scenes are more romantic than a sun-streaked bedroom opening onto a terrace set for breakfast. But the sunshine and leafy terrace are only two of many romantic attributes in this room in rural France. Huge, ancient beams recalling a rustic history contrast with light, pretty textiles, while a daybed invites cool rest away from the afternoon heat. The bedroom was converted from a near-ruined *bergerie* by Anna and Kyrle Simond.

ANTIQUE ORIGINS

This is an inventively designed room with classical antecedents. Mario Ascione's origins are steeped in the Hellenistic world of Pompeii and Ercolano, and these roots are manifest in the forms, colours and arrangement of his first-floor flat in London. The room was previously fairly typical of its kind, but the shape has been made more interesting by the insertion of an arch which gives a sense of separation between the more Pompeiian area and the Renaissance area. Apart from its obvious elegance, the arch instills the room with an air of mystery: the visitor cannot take in the entire scene at a single glance, and, inevitably, he or she is curious to know what decorative impedimenta hides round the corner. The pilasters to either side of the chimneypiece are further practical and decorative devices. One conceals the plumbing; the other was added for symmetry. The dado, painted with *trompe l'oeil* tassels and drapery by Tony Walford, has romantic echoes of an anteroom in an ancient Italian palace. The grey-painted frieze was designed to balance the room's proportions.

A MAGICAL DRAMA

Few London drawing-rooms can be more eccentric than this converted 50-foot studio with soaring ceiling and balcony. For Hannerle Dehn, the eccentricity of the place is what first attracted her. She fell for its special sense of timelessness and magic, the sort of magic one associates with ancient, faded palaces in Venice. She could imagine it dimly lit by candles, with crumbling gesso walls, painted furniture and lots of old silks. The room is now much as she had envisaged it, complete with gessoed walls which look at least a century old. Using her skills as a restorer and painter of decorative antique furniture, Hannerle Dehn has created a magical, memorable drama.

IN A CONVERTED GRANARY

This drawing-room is in a converted granary, part of an early-nineteenth-century manor-house complex in Wiltshire. Owner-decorator Peter Saunders has drawn colour right up to the apex in order to emphasize the loftiness and 'roundness' of the room. The height is further emphasized by the paired pillars to either side of the door which are used as giant pedestals. The furniture is a happy blend of antique continental and English styles.

NEW USE, NEW LIGHT

In a previous incarnation, this top-lit studio-style room was probably a billiards room. Originally, it would have been decorated in a heavy-handed manner, but now it has something of the air of a contemporary art gallery – which is appropriate, as its owner, Bob Lawrence, has a gallery specializing in early twentieth-century art and artefacts. The walls have been ragged and rolled in subdued shades of pink and grey by Jeff Sturkey. The strange and interesting floor markings are the result of a reaction from the old copper nails when the oak boards were bleached.

A LYRICAL EXPOSITION

Decorating and furnishing an oval room is, inevitably, more problematical than coping with a room with straight walls. For a start, how does one position the furniture? The answer can be seen in this lyrical salon in a house decorated by Tom Parr of Colefax & Fowler and Gerard Bach. Furniture with straight backs or sides is placed in the centre of the room, while furniture around the perimeter has either been specially made to fit the curve – as in the chintz-covered sofas – or has rounded outlines which 'touch' the walls without needing to align with them. These rounded pieces include circular tables, buttoned armchairs and gilded pedestals supporting lamps. All these elements are arranged symmetrically which suits the room's refined classical character. Curiously, this room is in an eighteenth-century rotunda in Switzerland, probably designed by an Italian architect but based on plans in John Plaw's *Rural Architecture* published in England in 1785. (See, too, pages 114–115 and 210–211).

ENRICHED FORM

Most new extensions to
quirky, old buildings lack the
interest, character and vitality
of the original house, but this
drawing-room addition in
Gloucestershire cannot be

faulted. The new room has a
striking, even majestic,
form, thanks to the height and
design of the ceiling. The
height gives the room a
marvellously airy quality and

provides scope for a grand
decorative treatment. Enriched
with gilded mouldings, the
ceiling has a central rose and
four corner decorations. The
walls are dragged in pale
terracotta-pink, a sympathetic
background for the eclectic

choice of furniture and
objects. Knowledgeable
selection is the strength of this
room. Nothing is predictable
but everything is well chosen
– and there is no fear of
combining old and new,
simple and ornate.

CHANGED CHARACTER

When this sitting-room in Cape Cod was built just over twenty years ago, it had a suspended plasterboard ceiling and looked decidedly conventional. After the plasterboard was ripped out, the room took on an entirely new character, one that is altogether more unusual and impactful. The limed beams create strong overhead patterns, but, thanks to their pale colour, are not overpowering. The creamy colour-scheme and open style of furnishing enhance the impression of space and light.

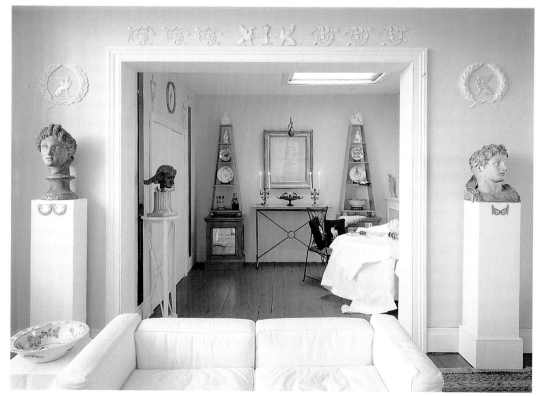

STUDIO CLASSICISM

Mary Goodwin's scheme for her home in an 1890s artist's studio in London emphasizes its special attributes of light and space. The scheme gives a definitively classical atmosphere and highlights the room's strong architectural lines. The oxidized copper-green colour was based on the drawing-room of Lansdowne House, designed by Robert Adam for the Earl of Bute in the 1760s and now on display in the Philadelphia Museum of Art. This homage to Robert Adam is underscored by the gilt and plaster mouldings of griffons, sphinxes, wreaths and vases cast from the original Adam moulds. A display cabinet transforms an awkward part of the studio into an attractive area for a group of eighteenth- and nineteenth-century ceramics. More ceramics are displayed in obelisks in an ante-room, used as a dining-area, which opens off the main room.

The focus of the overall scheme is the collection of casts of eighteenth-century sculpture which provide dramatic accents.

Grander windows

Open any book on interior decoration published, say, twenty years ago, and you will note that most of the curtain treatments were restrained to the point of anonymity. Curtains, bereft of trimmings, were hung either from plain, plastic tracks or from simple wooden poles. There was hardly a pelmet in sight, except for a few pieces of flat, stiffened fabric cut straight along the bottom edge. Only the most traditional of traditionalists were still hanging elaborate drapery. But, in the nineteen-eighties, all that restraint has been thrown out of the window. Windows in even quite ordinary rooms are now festooned and draped in a manner which would not have looked out of place at the height of the Victorian era. Textiles are once again very chic; you can't have too many or too much of them. Rooms are now brimming with fabrics in a multitude of patterns and colours. Cushions, old rugs, shawls and fancy curtains are *de rigueur*.

Curtains have become more than just panels of fabric used to screen the windows. They are important decorative features in their own right, crucial to the entire scheme of things. Drapery is now so significant that there are often several layers of curtains at a single window – first, blinds; then under curtains; and, finally, dress curtains which are never drawn. This layered effect is seen in the library on page 153, where outer curtains of patterned fabric are looped over handsome lion-mask medallions, while the straight under-curtains – those which actually draw – are of plain blue fabric to match the walls.

The length of curtains is another interesting phenomenon. Now, it is often so exaggerated that the fabric sweeps onto the floor and spreads out in huge fans. This sounds heavy and ponderous but it need not be, as witness the pale, creamy room on page 158. The colour-scheme in this double drawing-room derives from the fine Aubusson rug, combining soft, muted pinks and ivory-beige. The curtains are heavily lined and have long 'trains' and cabbage bows, but the plainness of the fabric and the light colour ensure that they are luxurious rather than oppressive.

The most spectacular of all the curtain treatments seen in this chapter are those by Clare Austin-Little on pages 142 and 156. Not everyone could live with such dramatic, complicated creations, combining antique and modern textiles, but they certainly reflect the present preoccupation with curtains and drapes.

The curtain treatment in this three-bay drawing-room is flattering to the panelling of the walls as well as to the windows. Pelmets of diaphanous silk are draped from central medallions and held to either side of the windows by bows. The curtains are of paler silk, the same fabric being used for simple swags across the top of the windows.

WELL DRESSED

The two windows in this drawing-room present a real problem because they are dissimilar in construction and lack symmetry. In order to mask the differences and to improve the proportions, interior decorator Sue Rathbone decided to abandon the idea of conventional curtains and pelmets and opt, instead, for festoons behind heavy, contrast-lined dress curtains. The scalloped shape of the festoons echoes the swagged drapery of the dress curtains and softens the rather harsh architecture of the windows. The treatment is appropriately luxuriant in a late-Victorian house and contributes to the 'weight' of the decoration whilst unifying both ends of the room.

DRAMATIC IMPORTANCE

In this drawing-room decorated by Clare Austin-Little, the curtain treatment is of dramatic importance. It is the focal-point, the *raison d'être*, of the room's entire decorative scheme. The pelmets have been painted with crackle-effect varnish, then treated with a glaze to give an antique appearance. Swags of damask, the same as that used for the dress curtains, have been applied to the pelmets, caught into cabbage bows at the corners. The under-curtains are of taffeta, and the *passementerie* is antique. This sort of theatrical drapery may not be for the faint-hearted but, indisputably, it transports a room into a new realm.

A SUPPLE SIMPLICITY

Artist Graham Rust is a natural, instinctive designer whose rooms exude harmony and well-being. Light in tone, yet warm in spirit, the colour-scheme of this L-shaped drawing-room was based on the colours of the sandstone rock formations of Petra, the mysterious classical city of antiquity in Jordan, where Graham Rust spent several months painting the temples and landscape. The rocks combine an earthy palette of yellow, beige, pink, white and black, all of which are represented in the room and are also seen in the painting above the sofa which depicts the treasury at Petra. The curtain treatment is a combination of festoons and straight-hanging drapes in palest beige edged with terracotta-pink. The arrangement is supple and graceful. At the wider end of the room, the wall between the windows is mirrored.

A FLUENT INTERPLAY

The windows in this
sitting-room have sufficient
height to take deeply swagged
drapery with fan edging and
elegant tails. Fixed at the
centres and sides of simple
rods, the drapery falls in soft
festoons, while the curtains,
gracefully looped over
ormolu tiebacks, continue the
fluent interplay of curves.

Eschewing gaudy trimmings
and contrasting fripperies, the
window treatment, though
elaborate, has a dignified
reserve. The sumptuous
golden-pink silk was chosen to
complement the subdued
tones of the Aubusson rug.
The room was decorated and
furnished with advice from
André de Cacqueray.

SWAGS AND PEDIMENTS

In this intimate, fabric-lined sitting-room, decorated by Nicholas Haslam, not only is there a pelmet at the window but also atop the bookcases recessed to either side of the chimneypiece. The bookcase pelmets in striped silk are wittily pediment-like in their design. (Incidentally, the curious use of parchment dust-wrappers on the books was copied from the eighteenth-century Stranof Library in Prague.) At the window, the dress curtains of green linen are paired with striped working curtains caught back with Italian stringing. The pelmet is swagged below the gathered curtain heading. Folding glass doors, lined with white muslin, lead into the dining-room which is illustrated overleaf.

ECHOES OF MALMAISON

The inspiration for this dining-room, designed by Nicholas Haslam, was drawn from Malmaison, the home of the Empress Josephine. The panelled effect on the walls and the Imperial motifs on the dado were painted by *trompe l'oeil* artist Sarah Jansen. The French influence is also manifest in the marble chimneypiece, the Louis-XVI bust of an actress and in the basket-weave chairs with their vivid green chintz 'hats' and squabs. The same chintz can be seen in the pelmet, an elaborate but lighthearted arrangement of white muslin fanning out from a central rosette and edged with green-and-white silk. Black fringe with gold tassels adds the final touch of theatre.

A SINGLE ENTITY

The two, full-height windows in this library overlooking a London square have been treated as a single entity. A black-and-gilt pelmet board, extending across the full width of the room, is hung with continuous drapery caught into pleats. Dress curtains, held back by lion-masks, are made of chintz, while 'working' curtains are of plain blue fabric to match the walls. The pelmet is extra-deep to suit the high ceiling. This splendid and vigorous room is the work of designer Brian Juhos.

DUO-TONE SILKS

The two ends of this double drawing-room have rugs and upholstery based on different colour-schemes – one uses greens and yellows, the other reds and blues – but the same rich, cream wall finish and distinctive curtain treatment unifies both areas. The walls have been coated with hot wax tinted with burnt siena, resulting in a glowing translucence which admirably becomes the diverse paintings.

The duo-tone curtains prove that a commanding effect can be realized without ostentatious pelmets and headings. Here, memorability is guaranteed by plain silk in ravishingly different colours.

ELABORATE ENSEMBLE

The prolific use of textiles is typical of Clare Austin-Little's style of interior decoration. Here, the window bay is swathed in a complicated arrangement of antique Aubusson pelmet, side festoons and taffeta curtains. The layered grandeur and interesting combination of rich fabrics gives the ensemble something of the character of a grand court costume. An imaginative array of textiles is also used for the cushions and round table. The latter has a floor-length cloth of black taffeta – chosen to co-ordinate with the black of the lacquered chest – encircled by taut swags of fabric which matches the sofa.

LUXURIOUS DISTINCTION

The design of these curtains is extravagant and weighty but the material itself is plain and light. Made of simple cream silk, the curtains are exaggeratedly long and heavily lined, sweeping the floor in generous folds. The swagged and tailed pelmets are lined in a deeper beige which tones with the pleated edging, braid and tassels. The unstinted arrangement softens the large areas of glazing and has a luxurious distinction without being oppressive. Unlike many rooms with traditional furniture, paintings and books, this room, decorated by Sisi Edmiston, has an appealing lightness. The colour-scheme was based on the muted pinks and creams of the large Aubusson rug.

En-suite

An *en-suite* bedroom and bathroom is no longer merely a question of layout – it is also a question of integrated interior decoration. Bathroom design, once the province solely of architects, has been taken up – and dressed up – by interior decorators. Interior decorators are treating bathrooms as comfortable decorative spaces, decked out with soft furnishings and even free-standing antique furniture. Gone is the institutional look with its minimal decoration and dreary, hard finishes. Now we have bathrooms which match up to the bedrooms they adjoin. If the bedroom is curtained with floral chintz and hung with prints, then so, too, is the bathroom. If the bedroom is a sophisticated scheme of marble and mirror, as seen at right, then so is the bathroom. The bathroom is now a truly pleasant room to linger in and enjoy rather than just a functional area to be used for the minimum possible time.

The most obvious trend in current bathroom design is the nostalgic look. Old baths and basins are being restored or copied; Edwardian-style taps are more popular than modern ones. And space is now considered well apportioned, not wasted, when given over to a bathroom. There was a time when the *en-suite* bathroom was the smallest room in the house, squeezed into the corner of the bedroom. Now, people are often prepared to sacrifice a second bedroom for a bathroom.

Nostalgia and space, then, are important features of today's bathrooms. Consider the bathroom on page 175 and you will see the model bathroom of the nineteen-eighties. Pretty, sybaritic and spacious, it looks just right in a country-house setting but is also the ideal of many town-dwellers. The curtains are as fetching as those in the bedroom; there is a rug as well as fitted carpet; and, needless to say, there is a roll-top bath. The bath is placed centrally in the room – surely the ultimate spatial indulgence.

But the most truly integrated bedroom and bathroom is in Homayoun Mazandi's house shown on page 166. The two spaces are open to one another, and the interior decoration throughout is consistent: soft, cloud-like paintwork and creamy-white textiles. The scheme was designed to echo the panoramic view of the sky and river seen from the windows and to allow Homayoun Mazandi to enjoy her surroundings, especially her antique furniture and favourite *objets d'art*, even while taking a bath.

Blue marble and mirror are the shared leitmotifs in this precise, sleek bedroom and bathroom in Paris designed by architect, Raymond. In the bedroom, marble is used for the continuous bedhead and bedside table. In the bathroom, the same marble forms the bath and surround to the basin. Both rooms also share a similar curtain treatment.

ALL-OVER PATTERN

This bedroom and bathroom in Victoire and Patrick de Montal's house in southern France are all-over patterned in the typically French manner. Fabric printed with pink and red peonies lines the walls, covers the beds, curtains the windows and upholsters the furniture. Both rooms are furnished more like sitting-rooms than purely functional spaces for sleeping and bathing. Everywhere there are pictures, decorative objects and family mementoes. Even the shells and rocks on the bath surround and on the hearth in the bathroom are reminders of family holidays. With its oriental rugs, marble chimneypiece and good wooden furniture, the bathroom is especially unusual and cosy. A large panel of mirror above the bath creates the illusion of width in what is a comparatively narrow room.

THE COLOURS OF SPRING

The English country-house look is often associated with clutter – lots of furniture, pattern piled on pattern, pictures and objects in profusion. This bedroom, however, is comparatively sparely decorated and furnished, yet it still manages to look unmistakably English. The colour scheme here and in the adjoining bathroom is light and spring-like: primrose-yellow walls, green-trellis carpet and hydrangea-patterned chintz. The vaulted ceiling in the bathroom was a pleasant surprise uncovered during a recent refurbishment. The interestingly-designed cupboards have doors with inset panels of wire mesh in front of pleated fabric.

CONTINUITY AND SPACE

For Homayoun Mazandi, the wish to be able to enjoy her surroundings, even while bathing, was paramount in influencing her decision to leave the bathroom open to the bedroom rather than separate it off. The two spaces take up the entire top floor of her London house overlooking the Thames. When she commissioned Hamel Cooke to paint the walls, part of the brief was to bring the effect of the panoramic view of the sky and river into the room, thus creating an impression of continuity and space. The panoply of blues is off-set by creamy-whites and black.

ATTIC HARMONY

This honey-toned bedroom and bathroom form an L-shaped arrangement beneath the eaves of Victoire and Patrick de Montal's house in France (see, too, pages 162–163). Massive beams evoke the ancient lineage of the house, while skylights have been recently – and discreetly – introduced to bring daylight to these attic spaces. Antique furniture and pale-wood surrounds to the bath and basins give a sense of tradition and unity. A built-in look has been deliberately avoided in the bathroom: there are free-standing towel rails, occasional chairs and a fabric-covered screen hung with a collection of miniatures and family photographs. The screen, though decorative in its own right, is a practical means of concealing the WC.

BLUE ON BLUE

Smartness and prettiness are often incompatible, but not in this bedroom, designed by Henrietta Gelber, where both qualities are well in evidence. The walls are prettily finished with a soft, cloud-like effect in cream, blue and grey. The same palette – though the blue is stronger – is seen in the Chinoiserie-pattern fabric used for all the curtaining and for the bathroom walls. In the bedroom, the pelmets are smartly edged with plain blue pleated fabric, which is also used to outline the bedhead. Lace-edged pillows and a linen bedcover provide crisp, white contrasts.

CURVILINEAR THEMES

Colour and curves unify this masculine-style bedroom and bathroom in an early-nineteenth-century house in Switzerland (see 130–131 and 176–177) During the recent restoration of the room, the original treatment of the walls was exposed. This showed large, plain, oval panels, probably intended for murals which were never executed. These panels now form dramatic, oculus-like shapes within a scheme of Pompeiian-red and grey-blue paintwork. The bed is recessed in an alcove, as is the bath, a free-standing, roll-top design on paw feet.

FLOWER BOWER

A passion for gardens and flowers prompted the choice of fabric in this bedroom decorated by Nessa O'Neill of Beaudesert. The pattern and application of the fabric is very feminine, combining pinks and greens, frills and swags. Pictures, cushions and plants take up the floral theme – a theme continued in the bathroom where the chintz inspired the stencilling by Felicity Binyon and Liz Macfarlane. Generously proportioned and not overlooked, the bathroom affords the luxury of placing the bath centrally beneath the window onto the garden.

RECALLING THE PAST

Trompe l'oeil wallpaper simulating draped fabric encircles this bedroom in a rotunda in Switzerland (see, too, pages 130–131). Recalling the nineteenth century, it is an appropriate foil for deeply-upholstered furniture. In the bathroom, the floral carpet is used unconventionally up the side of the bath surround.

Flexible stripes

Stripes are the most primitive of patterns, yet they are inherently satisfying and have universal application. They suit many different styles of decoration, obligingly bridging the gap between plain and ornate, sophisticated and naive. They co-exist happily with most other patterns and, unlike more elaborate confections, they can also be used in conjunction with plain surfaces without any feeling of domination. A variety of effects can be gained by using stripes in different widths and in different combinations of colours. A single-colour stripe on a white background always looks smart and fresh, while stripes in two tones of the same colour are more restful, especially in period settings.

Stripes were particularly popular for fabrics during the early nineteenth century, either in the form of simple, alternating bands of colours, or as a background for other, more intricate patterns, possibly sprays of flowers. Stripes of one sort or another have retained their popularity ever since but, recently, there has been a superabundance of them. Every manufacturer of wallpapers and fabrics now produces extensive ranges of striped and striped-background designs. These patterns suit today's wish for an enriched style of decoration combined with a sense of tradition and order.

The striped rooms in this chapter span a country-house idyll near Bath and a tailored, masculine study in Paris. These disparate settings illustrate the adaptability of stripes. In the former, on page 186, a self-coloured wallpaper provides a warm background against which many other patterns are superimposed. The stripes have a unifying effect whilst being a sympathetic foil for antique furniture and pictures. In the study on page 182, the effect is much crisper and more graphic, even though much of the furniture is also antique or antique-inspired. Here, striped fabric is used for curtains and walls alike, giving an all-round cohesion.

Another all-round application of striped fabric is seen in the dramatically-tented dining-room on page 188. This is a merry room, designed to counteract the potential gloom of an internal space with a low ceiling and virtually no natural light. Stripes work particularly well in this situation. Their verticality gives the room height and helps to define the shape of the tented roof.

This country-house drawing-room has a light, joyful character thanks to the unaffected style of decoration by Carrie Naylor-Leyland. The broad stripes of the wallpaper, sophisticated and cheerful, have presence without being intrusive and link the room's various plain and patterned textiles.

WARM COLOURS AND TEXTURES

This room posed two potential problems for interior designer Karen Armstrong of Pavilion Designs: a low ceiling and a cool, easterly aspect. Both snags have been successfully overcome by lining the walls with a smart, vertical-striped fabric in a warm shade of pink and by incorporating a lively mix of textiles for the furnishings. Working closely with the owners, Karen Armstrong devised a scheme which deliberately eschewed an over-coordinated look. She has used varied textures – velvet, linen, wool and chintz – while maintaining a careful balance of large and small patterns.

TAILORED BACKGROUND

Striped fabric stretched tautly over the walls in this study in Paris, designed by Claude Vicario, is a neat, tailored background for a sky-painted screen by American artist, Robert Davison, and for eighteenth-century Piranesi architectural engravings. The latter are unusually mounted between two sheets of glass which extend beyond the prints and are framed in black. Other unorthodox features in the room include the over-scaled Murano vases on the chimneypiece and the eclectic choice of furniture. An Art Deco desk, a pivoting games table (designed by Claude Vicario) and a *faux-*porphyry Directoire tallboy are of different generations but live in harmony.

ESTABLISHED ORDER

An established, club-like atmosphere has been created by Carole Langton and Virginia White in this dining-room in a flat in London. The gilt of the handsome picture frames, hung from brass chains and poles, looks particularly splendid against the dignified, self-striped fabric used for the walls and curtains. The silken sheen of the fabric gives life to a setting which concentrates on deep tones and traditional furniture. The circular mahogany table, standing on a square rug, is compatible with the room's square proportions. The curvilinear backs of the sturdy Hepplewhite chairs counteract the room's comparatively severe lines without appearing frivolous. The arrangement and choice of furniture and furnishings is highly ordered, avoiding fussy or exaggerated detail. The red edging to the curtains is the narrowest of fringes but provides a valuable link with the colours of the chair covers, rug and paintings.

TRADITIONAL YELLOW

Yellow is hard to beat in climates where sunshine is unpredictable. It generates visual warmth and accords especially well with traditional furnishings. This drawing-room in a handsome stone manor-house near Bath was decorated with the help of Tom Parr of Colefax & Fowler and uses a two-tone yellow paper above a dado dragged in off-white. The carpet combines both colours and underpins seating with various, complementary covers. Everything is organized yet not constrained. Symmetry is seen in the grouping of the furniture, but the symmetry is not repressive, thanks to soft cushions, flowers, books and magazines.

TENTED SOLUTION

In a room with a low ceiling and virtually no natural light, how can one detract from the gloomy feeling of dining underground? This was the conundrum confronting Monika Apponyi when she redecorated a house in Chelsea where a kitchen extension had caused the dining-room to become an internal space without windows. The answer she came up with was to shallow-tent the space in a blue-and-white striped cotton finished with red braid. The alcoves to either side of the chimneypiece are curtained to suggest greater depth to the room, while the opening to the kitchen is also curtained. Low-voltage lighting creates a pleasant, daylight effect.

GENTLE PAINTWORK

Although the broad stripes in this London drawing-room look highly regimented, they are, in fact, hand-painted, giving a subtler, gentler finish than printed paper. The blue is picked up by a narrow band of colour between the white cornice and frieze. The pelmet arrangement is a pretty combination of self-striped fabric and blue-and-white fringing, the graceful, serpentine form softening the room's verticality. Blue is often maligned as a 'cold' colour, but when juxtaposed with red and gilt, as here, it comes alive. The room was designed by Jane Churchill; the specialist paintwork was by David Mendl.

COLOURFULLY ECLECTIC

This dining-room is far removed from those cold, inhibiting dining-rooms one so often comes across in town houses. This is a casual, comfortable and enjoyable affair, mildly eccentric and distinctly jolly. The background to the eclectic collection of pictures – ranging from a series of costume prints to an impressive canvas of cherries by Tony Hambro – is a splendid raspberry-red striped wallpaper, its strong colour and bold definition acting as a disciplined foil for a mass of textiles and cosy clutter. Lengths of silk damask are casually looped over pelmet poles and tied with tassels and rosettes, while a gold-threaded silk scarf is draped over the back of the sofa and tied in huge knots over the arms. The room was decorated by Nathalie Hambro, whose passion for stripes can also be seen on pages 196–197.

JAUNTILY STRUCTURED

This strongly delineated room
in an early Georgian
town-house was decorated by
Rosemary Hamilton around
a collection of Biedermeier
furniture. Striped wallpaper

and curtains provide a
structured yet jaunty backdrop
for the quirky outlines of the
seating and handsome bureau.
Instead of placing four
matching chairs round the

small, circular table,
Rosemary Hamilton has made
the less predictable choice of
two, distinctly different
pairs: one has arms, the other
has curious, fan-shaped backs
and wooden seats. Against the
wall opposite the window is
a sofa covered in the same
fabric as the chairs. The
predominant colour
throughout is blue. This not
only looks well with
pale-wood furniture but
complements the marine
themes of the paintings.

LIVELY AND ORIGINAL

The grey wallpaper in this sitting-room by Nathalie Hambro is just right for her bold choice of furniture and decorative objects. Its restrained colouring does not fight with the furnishings but, equally, the broadness of the stripes ensures that the paper is not swamped. Indeed, it is a masterly foil for the huge, colourful kelim which covers virtually the entire length of the room. The room is an extraordinary mixture of styles and scale – but it has undeniable *éclat*. To either side of the chimneypiece are huge French bronze ormolu sconces; seating ranges from a nineteenth-century daybed to a double chair by Ron Arad made from two 1940s car seats in a chrome frame; fabrics are printed, woven and embroidered in a miscellany of patterns. Altogether, a lively and original assembly.

LINEAR FINESSE

Stripes need not be strident to make a decorative statement. In this top-floor bedroom, red-and-white wallpaper has a delicacy and finesse which marries well with the fresh, floral chintz and provides an unassertive but far from bland background for pictures. In order to be able to hang pictures on all the walls, the sloping window-wall was straightened, creating deep window alcoves. The curtains are edged with a narrow band of red, as are the lampshades. The walls, too, are outlined with a sliver of red Petersham. The room was decorated by Anthony and Valerie Evans of Top Layer.

Dining with panache

The history of the dining-room is a closer reflection of social mores and attitudes than any other room in the house. Rooms used exclusively and regularly for formal dining hardly existed until the late seventeenth century. Before then, meals were taken in the Great Hall, or tables and chairs were set up in a small, informal parlour. Even in the eighteenth century, meals were often taken in whatever room was convenient. The Victorians made much of their dining-rooms as a means of displaying wealth and status but, in our own time, the existence of a separate dining-room has been challenged by lack of space and a more casual lifestyle. The open-plan mentality of the nineteen-sixties led to the dining-table being absorbed into the living-room or 'family' kitchen. But, latterly, there has been a noticeable and welcome trend for separate rooms for dining. This makes entertaining far more enjoyable – providing, of course, that the room is decorated in an unpompous, interesting manner. Alas, pomposity is all too common a fault. Almost everyone must have suffered the doleful experience of eating in an impeccably-furnished dining-room which is so lacking in intimacy that even the most extrovert of guests is hushed and downcast. Conversely, there are rooms in which none of the fabrics match, the chairs are old and worn, and the china past its prime, but the atmosphere is happy and inspiring. Getting the decoration of the dining-room right, then, does not depend on perfectly co-ordinated fabrics or priceless furniture. It has more to do with personal style and originality.

There is something to be said for using rich colours in the dining-room, as these look warm and inviting. Lighting, too, is important. And as dining-rooms are used for limited periods, fantasy and romance can also play a part in their decoration. The Swiss dining-room on page 210 gives the illusion of eating in a classical landscape; the stencilling on the walls of the room on page 202 was derived from an exotic rug; the ceiling of the room on page 218 simulates a sky with scurrying clouds . . . these are the sort of decorative fantasies which ensure that the dining-room is an entertaining room in every sense.

This glistening dining-room, designed by the owner in conjunction with Karen Armstrong of Pavilion Designs, has something of the quality of a theatre set. A dramatic arrangement of silk taffeta is swagged across the top of the window reveal and falls in deep folds to either side. The walls and shutters were marbled by Corinne Peers de Niewburg to counterfeit four different types of stone, creating an extravagantly panelled effect above and below the dado rail.

STENCILLED STYLE

The initial idea for the fresh colour-scheme in this dining-room in London, designed by Mimmi O'Connell, derived from the blue-and-white porcelain. The addition of a dhurrie rug prompted the secondary idea for the stencilling of the walls by Jo Monoprio and Clare Stourton. Now, the same geometric pattern – complete with Greek-key border – is seen on walls and floor alike. It is a brilliantly simple means of giving character to a bland basement room. The central motif of the dhurrie pattern is terracotta-coloured which, at night, radiates a warm glow.

DRAWN FROM DELFT

The decoration of this dining-room was inspired by the collection of Delft plates which now punctuates the walls. The small scale and regular repeat of the Gothic wallpaper, specially printed to match the blue of the Delftware, enhance the free style of painting seen on the plates. The dado and woodwork have been marbled by Malcolm Connell in a soft grey-blue, while the furnishing of the room is deliberately simple: a circular table, a set of early Regency chairs – and no carpet.

ART AND ILLUSION

Art and illusion have been successfully employed to give this dining-room symmetry and a sense of light. The right-hand window is pure fake, painted by Alex Dunhill to match the left-hand, real window, complete with glazing bars and curtains. The fabric of the curtains is printed with classical emperors' heads, an apposite foil for the classical architectural pictures. From the centre of the boldly compartmented ceiling hangs an eighteenth-century French bronze chandelier.

NAÏVE CHARM

The charm of this kitchen and dining-room, decorated by Elaine Wilson, can be ascribed to the naïve style of furniture and decorative objects. The eighteenth-century English dresser displays American and English spongeware. Above the chimneypiece hangs a primitive painting of a cow. The table, covered with a nineteenth-century American quilt, is partnered by rush-seated chairs. And, in keeping with the overall tenor, the floorboards have been left bare and the wall treatment kept simple.

IN AN ANTIQUE LANDSCAPE

Dining in this oval, vaulted room is like dining in a classical pavilion in an antique landscape. One wall is painted with a view of Vesuvius; another depicts Lac d'Averno. These tranquil evocations of a distant past date from the early nineteenth century and have recently been restored. The marquetry floor dates from the same period. The apse opposite the window is set out as a secondary dining-area, lined with close-gathered blue fabric.

RECOLLECTIONS OF SWEDEN

In Simon and Beata Gillow's dining-room, the intensity of the yellow walls, bordered by a simple grey frieze, recalls Swedish neo-classical decoration. This is appropriate on two counts: first, Beata's mother is Swedish and, second, the Gillows' house and fine collection of furniture have a strong neo-classical character throughout. In this room the furniture includes a set of late nineteenth-century German Biedermeier dining-chairs and sofa, and two English Regency sideboards. On the wall opposite the windows, the vast *Procession of Bacchus at the Time of the Vintage* by Blake Richmond hangs unframed, giving the effect of a fresco. Between the windows hangs a family portrait by Franz von Lenbach. The splendid curtains came originally from a French chateau and, by happy chance, needed virtually no alteration. The elegant stairs, designed by Beata Gillow, lead up to the kitchen.

A VARIETY OF SOURCES

The American owners of this London dining-room are international in their lifestyle and eclectic in their tastes. Their dramatically-decorated dining-room, decorated with advice from Anthony Ormiston, uses furniture and effects from a variety of sources: the chairs are Portuguese, the chandelier is Russian, the leather screen Italian, the glassware French and the dinner service English ironstone. By chance, the pattern of the antique screen is very similar to that of the fabric used for the curtains and portière to the hallway, though the screen was a later addition. The eighteenth-century silk used for the tablecloth is a sumptuous centrepiece.

CONSERVATORY GOTHIC

Eighteenth- and
early-nineteenth-century
Gothic is one of Britain's most
appealing domestic building
styles, especially when
adapted to small country
houses, garden buildings and
conservatories. This Gothic
conservatory is new but it
echoes the pointed-arch
windows of the 1820s Gothic
lodge it adjoins. Used as a
dining-room, it is furnished in
a more sophisticated manner
than most conservatories.
The chairs are comfortable
and stylish, while the fabrics
have busy patterns rivalling
the filigree tangle of plant life.
The interior was designed by
George Spencer. (See, too,
pages 20–21.)

THEATRICAL FUSION

The Paris dining-room of the renowned fabric designer, Manuel Canovas, and his wife, Catherine, is a dazzling fusion of simplicity and grandeur. The high ceiling is painted with scurrying clouds; the cornice and dado are vigorously and splendidly marbled; the walls are lined with moiré in old-rose pink.

The paintings are few but dramatic. Furniture, too, is kept to a minimum: a set of painted chairs, an oval table with a long, damask cloth, and two fabric-draped side-tables. The ambience is theatrical and stimulating, conveying an air of expectancy, like a set waiting for the play to begin.

KEEPING IN SCALE

A table big enough to seat sixteen rarely looks comfortable in a domestic setting. It either smacks of the boardroom or of the school dining-room. In this dining-room, the problem has been overcome by using two smaller tables. Covered with embroidered cloths, and partnered by *faux* bamboo chairs, each table not only looks decorative but in scale with its setting. The room's colour-scheme is based on lime-green and stone. The walls have been sponged to give a stone-like appearance, and the cupboards and chimneypiece are painted in the same tone. Above the chimneypiece hangs a still-life by Antonio Viudes, while the arch-topped alcoves display a collection of pre-Columbian sculpture.

SHEER FANTASY

The decoration of this room in a late-Victorian mansion flat, devised by Rawya Mansour, is sheer fantasy, inspired by a pair of French seventeenth-century wooden columns. These are now central to the scheme which combines specialist paint effects by Folkart and murals by American theatrical artist, Ward Veazey. An ornamental birdcage on the window-sill and a clipped box tree introduce architectural and sculptural elements.